Grazing

❦ *Grazing*

❦ ❦ ❦ ❦ ❦ ❦ ❦ ❦ ❦

Poems by Ira Sadoff

University of Illinois Press
Urbana and Chicago

Manufactured in the United States of America

P 5 4 3 2 1

This book is printed on acid-free paper.

Library of Congress Cataloging-in-Publication Data
Sadoff, Ira.
Grazing : poems / by Ira Sadoff.
p. cm.
ISBN 0-252-06737-1 (acid-free paper)
I. Title.
PS3569.A26 G73 1998
811'.54—ddc21 98-8950

CIP

PS
3569
.A26
G73
1998

Acknowledgments

Earlier versions of some of these poems have appeared in the following magazines and anthologies:

Alaska Review: "Delirious"
American Poetry Review: "Before and After," "The Depression," "Eternity," "Grazing," "I Like Ike," "An Improbable Delirium," "The Inner Life," "Izzy," "The Rapture," "Standard Time," "There's No Rigor like the Old Rigor," "Time and Space," and "Vivaldi"
Antaeus: "My Mother's Funeral"
Black Moon: "The Martyrs"
Boulevard: "When I Come Home"
Colorado Review: "On the Day of Nixon's Funeral," "Overheard," "The Quake," and "Solitude Etude"
Cream City Review: "Bud Powell at the Club Montmarte, 1961"
Denver Quarterly: "February"
The Harper American Literature, ed. Robert Atwan, Martha Banta, Justin Kaplan, David Minter, Donald McQuade, Robert Stepto, Cecilia Tichi, and Helen Vendler (New York: HarperCollins, 1994): "My Mother's Funeral"
Introspections, ed. Robert Pack and Jay Parini (Hanover: University Press of New England, 1997): "Solitude Etude"
Kenyon Review: "A Missed Opportunity" and "At the Grand Canyon"
Michigan Quarterly Review: "At the Movies"

The Movies: Texts, Receptions, Exposures, ed. Lawrence Goldstein and Ira
   Konigsburg (Ann Arbor: University of Michigan Press, 1997): "At the
   Movies"
New Republic: "Against Whitman" and "Biographical Sketch"
Ontario Review: "Selma"
Paris Review: "Language" and "On the Job"
Prairie Schooner: "The Horse Wanted Sugar" and "In the Dream"
The Pushcart Prize Anthology, ed. Bill Henderson (Wainscott: Pushcart,
   1997): "Time and Space"
TriQuarterly: "I Like Waking Up"
Virginia Quarterly Review: "I Join the Sparrows" and "The Myelogram"
The Yearbook of American Verse, ed. Alan Pater (New York: Monitor, 1997):
   "At the Movies"

For Linda, Casey, and Julie
with love

Contents

🍃 Part 3

🌿 Part 1

Vesuvius don't talk—Etna don't— . . . One of them—
said a syllable—a thousand years ago, and Pompeii
heard it, and hid forever—she couldn't look the world
in the face afterward—I suppose—Bashful Pompeii!
"Tell you of the want"—you know what a leech is,
don't you—and you have felt the horizon haven't
you—and did the sea—never come so close as to make
you dance?

—Emily Dickinson

My Mother's Funeral

The rabbi doesn't say she was sly and peevish,
fragile and voracious, disheveled, voiceless and useless,
at the end of her very long rope. He never sat beside her
like a statue while radio voices called to her from God.
He doesn't say how she mamboed with her broom,
staggered, swayed, and sighed afternoons,
till we came from school to feed her. She never frightened *him*,
or bent to kiss him, sponged him with a fever, never held his hand,
bone-white, bolted doors, and shut the blinds. She never sent
roaches in a letter, he never saw her fall down stairs, dead sober.
He never watched her sweep and murmur, he never saw
spiderwebs she read as signs her life was over, long before
her frightened husband left, long before
they dropped her in a box, before her children turned
shyly from each other, since they never learned to pray.
If I must think of her, if I can spare her moment on the earth,
I'll say she was one of God's small sculptures,
polished to a glaze, one the wind blew off a shelf.

February

A mist appalls the windshield.
So I still see trees as moral lessons,
as I pass under them, shadowy and astute.

The glazed aspen branches hover.
Ice heats up and cracks, road tar steams
like some animal where the blush

of cheek is chilled by annunciation.
I cannot say her face was trauma driven.
I'm still saturated with her, taking in

her etched-in countenance, otherworldly,
enveloping, frightening, the face you can't see,
pressed against it. So how can you imagine

what it feels *like?* Their gravity suffices,
the sealed and straining torsos
of aspens, an affront to our high-pitched moans,

feverish with disarray. Our expressions
have too much God in them, too much cloud, too much
blood on nail, too much arrow, too much quiver.

When I Come Home

after the Xenia tornado of 1974

In Cincinnati the river is the color of nausea,
and in Xenia the tops of houses
have been taken off and rest in the river.

When I come home and she's not home,
the worry thickens, I think she must be sick
not to want me. I still have a picture

of that naked girl on fire in My Lai,
her arms high in the air, her hands
screaming, and behind her, her mother

waving a handkerchief on a stick. And behind them
the whole village running from their village,
napalm scorching their thatched huts to slag.

Xenia means friendship. Xenia means flower.
See what a name means.
To be afraid of Xenia is to be afraid of the other.

The sky is mud and thunder. The air is green,
thick with pollen, my wife and I swing on a porch swing,
listening to the frogs and crickets, thinking,

The elm tree is a thing of beauty. The elm tree's actually an oak,
but we can hear the stream unfurling.
We enjoy the wetness of it. The essence of it, dripping.

We are only twenty-one and twenty-two, singing.
I still have a picture of her, her arm
wrapped around my arm, her lips on my neck, pursed.

When I come home and she's not home,
the story of the world is not of interest. I am
speechless, going back there, to the four-room cabin

in the dense Ohio wood, still further back,
waiting to disappoint, failing to predict how to soothe.
The sick are nothing but plasma, whereas the healthy

play the saxophone and saturate the river.
The world is not as heavy as the door to my room, open.
She lost her wedding ring in the crack beneath the buckled floor,

so she's free. I think about fire dropped on a child,
the funnel spinning, coming closer, the sky white as knuckles,
a snow of splinters, how I'm behind the couch, waiting.

I can feel the blood rush in and my skin on fire.
To listen to my heart, you'd think we'd seized it, the music,
the state called rapture. Where the river runs in summer,

nothing but a few flies and stones to disturb it. The two of us
sitting and listening, unprepared for what comes next.
This is only a story, so I can say what I want. I can hold back

the ending for a moment, when I come home from school,
when we call out, when the bloody soldier burns away
attention span, when a helicopter wheels him off to heaven.

Time and Space

I made her cry in public. They were singing, uproariously,
nine of them, all couples, save my wife,
dabbing her cheek with a handkerchief. Our betrayals

had been mutual, deleterious, densely textured,
less suggestive of Diana than Orestes. Then I'd left.
But they made no allusion to that schism, love, so

their happy faces must have seemed to her like prisms
of Cezanne's. The meal was all fable and deflection,
a melody sung off-key. Still, there was no denying it,

the shifting chairs, sudden coughs, subjects changing
with great alacrity. Across the water I heard no sirens
sing, though the harp of veins and arteries surely

had been plucked, reddening her stricken face. If only
art could make our stories larger. Dear friends
spared me the news. Years later, a thoughtless stranger told me.

Solitude Etude

I spent years on my knees while she
got off before me, her eyes fluttering closed,
her mind several men away, their cocks
glistening spit and then, when twitching
turned to tedium (every night the same position)
she deigned to let me in, and waited patiently
for me to finish up. Shut up, I'm talking now.

And as I speak, some psycho with tattoos
drills McDonald's with his M-16. Killing children,
yes, and priests and Digital execs. Mothers, wives,
and daughters. Serial killers, mass murderers,
they're the latest chattel on the avenue. Curious:
we like them with one leg, eating gruel
from garbage cans—half-savage, pornographic beasts—

or else well-dressed boys with A's.
The neighbors said, *We fed him milk and cookies.*
I stood before that counter, waiting for my meal,
or used to stray behind my house in the flats, picking up
old toys soaked with mud. I longed for one small gem,
ruby or amethyst, a gift for her, to prove
I was more than a standing pond, the slick

wet granite of a shallow ditch. The night my wife
bedded down Nick Gonzales (why spare his name?)
I found the proof I needed playing pinball
at a truck stop in Wyoming: I'd never felt more lost,
more ashamed, more myself. A man my age
was on the next machine, praying
to bells and lights named for women's breasts.

Dry-mouthed and needle-pocked, half-hypnotized,
teary-eyed, swooning with a moan, he sang,
Oh mama, please don't bring me down.
Who's to blame? The Reverend Moon,
Sigmund Freud, Phil Donahue? Her brute
of a father, fucking his way through her mother
in his lover's voice (did I really lick her wrist)?
Movie sex, where a healthy buck will raise
his partner to the counter and stuff her
full of ammunition? Now they retrieve
the carcass of a child, his ninety-nine-cent meal

pressed to his chest. The killer's beside him,
handcuffed, arms behind his back,
overweight, expressionless, his face gone slack:

he brings me back to *Little America,*
that dank pisshole near Laramie, where I'd shake
the sleepless man whose fists are curled, who's snagged
on rage and blame, and in the morning, dress
and raise him up before the hotel mirror,
open the door on that mesmerizing, snow-capped
mountain range: jagged, treacherous, too slick to climb.

Standard Time

Winter was a vestibule, storing brooms
in closets, every sequence white with snow, hauling wood
in that embraceable wind. I'd like the world to be a room
in a poem, for obvious reasons. The ice was thin,
the stripped-down flesh oblivious. I had one thin coat
for protection. Could the snow drift still higher,
blocking my view? There was my marriage to look at, the war,
a friend dead of AIDS, a healthy baby for another,
all scars and snapshots (*Had I seen these before?*).

The door slammed our voices shut. But that was early.
We bombed a milk factory, that much I remember. Or was it later,
in summer? Mostly I remember holding Sascha's hand,
watching chained-up elephants—an intact family—
swaying in three-four time, making the best of it. Rodin
told Rilke, Flee from yourself. Go to the zoo. Just pay attention,
for Christ's sake. It could have been my wife. But all
the scraps and remnants splintered, everything so briefly shattered:
before I knew it I'd picked up a new pair of glasses,
the snow had stopped, and what I held in my hand,
a few snapped twigs and canvas sling of logs, was useless now.

The Horse Wanted Sugar

Sascha shivered where the mare'd licked her hand.
December, when things should be ending,
but Sascha picked up twigs and shriveled berries,
even tufts of frozen grass and invited them

to her palm, the horses. Did I wish she were mine?
Did I look into the wind that brushed our faces numb?
Did she show me the way to make them chew,
stroking their noses and singing nonsense tunes

in their ears? I could mention the stinging tears
and the whining that followed in a meadow
whose sole shelter was an old stone fence
and a mangled maple bent over a pond.

In a flash she wanted to be home where she belonged.
So I raised her on my shoulders and we galloped for a mile,
neighing and crying, till her father met us at the door.
I blew into her hand and hung her snowsuit in the closet.

"The horse wanted sugar," Sascha said. "But we fed him a leaf."

Before and After

I was too sick to leave the factory.
Out of work, feverish, weak—my head a cloud
but filled with ideas I scribbled down.
It was like a sex thing, only back and forth
between syllables. My brain flooded that sheen of blue
the sky pretends to be. I'd suffered a few losses. X and Y
had left me like a pocket, railing on the sixth floor of the depository.

Do you think we're important? The way we're mistreated matters?
Can you equate the strap on the back with the cults of Satan?
So embedded in us is our incessant pointlessness,
we keep going back to what kicked and scratched at us,
and yes there are a hundred corpses inside us, keeping us aclutter.

You know how we become stupid as we get older,
walking into a room for something—a set of keys,
a book, a change of clothes—and come back out wondering,
What was it, what was it? We want to figure things out,
how a particular thing died, who's to blame,
to pry open the flesh, holding up the vial of blood
a shade too dark to be ours, but also bringing ourselves close
to the fallen, reaping the air it breathed, trying to revive it.

We need someone to rescue us
from the sullen gatekeeper, the zipper over our mouths,
the bitter taste of licorice and clay, from decayed
shitholes like Troy, where in shoe factories
fathers and mothers slump over their hammers and tool-dyed leather
stamping out the urge to murder standing upright at the bar

speculating. No one wants to admit it:
the kenneled dogs bark their hysterical, circular cries
accompanied by the voices of screeching tires—
the overturned car is followed by the knife and saw
of the autopsy. That's why I can't bring you
to the blank spot, site of ruin, the deathbed
where everyone arrives before us, where we can watch
how white white is, how a voice pales, how ravenous we are
at the end. We want to hear about the before and after,
the sputtering venom, the slippages, the molten fluids
blackening the town. The staggering semblance of existence
stirring in the bowels, the sheer magma of it all. Like,

shots rang out from behind the knoll.

Instead you get a Twice-born muttering in tongues,
an easy target staggering down Montgomery: you can't help but brush
against the stench of his overcoat, the bristling madness
of his chin, and walking right behind him, don't worry, I'm taking notes,
I'm going to get us out of this: not with some cheap ceramic little Christ
or some promise we bob in the sea like a buoy in solution:
the man's my uncle, a snapshot I saw in a magazine, a composite sketch,
the six-year-old boy stamped on the milk carton,
the bullet, arc, and trajectory, the victim.

Biographical Sketch

To say she was seductive, paranoid, agoraphobic, repressed,
to say she had spindly dancer's legs, the eyes
of a cow, to say she had the voice of oil on a frying pan,
the skin of a comma, to say she loved azaleas,
her room was cluttered with cut-up articles
on Jesus' face in a tree, to say she heard the radio
before you plugged it in, to say the pond
where her father drowned never left her face
is to forget the pennies she picked up off the sidewalk,
her husband killing himself for a buck, is to forget
modern appliances appearing before her
pretending to be friends, but to say sex was a job,
a few jagged longings lagging behind duty
and expectation, a creature of her age, lacks immediacy
and hope, forgets the will, the individual
who manages to succeed by "hard work" and "imagination,"
is to forget the photograph in your hand is not
the one you knew: her words are borrowed murmurs,
like the black widows' dress made for so many,
is to refuse to see her eyes when you look most bereft,
is to touch her green lamb's wool sweater,
what's left of it, that shred of cloth that gave her color
and fervor, reflected in her eyes a glint and spark:
is to try to forget: she was guileless, frenzied, gone to waste.

On the Job

I support the animals' urge to survive.
So much for opinions. Slithering, writhing,
nosing my way through dirt, I can identify

with that. I joke to keep the system going.
So whatever the effect of clearing island fog
with concomitant deer nibbling berry bushes

at dusk, I keep my distance. I keep the home office
—pencil scratches, accommodating memos, bows—
yawning. But the gnawing animal stalks us,

keeps us feeding and feeling weak. García Lorca
once said, "When the moon rises, the heart feels
like an island in infinity." Who can improve on that?

My labor must mean something. The worn salt lick,
narrow paths and droppings in my meadow, velvet residue
of antlers, all are real enough. I keep the hunters out.

In the Dream

We launch from a city wharf an old canoe
through the drab and scabrous waters, water of dented cans
and hypodermics, of old brassieres and shaved hair,
water of dead flesh and fecal stench. My hands are oars

tangled in debris. We're headed for a picnic on a nearby isle
until I strike what must be an animal, because the bow
begins to knife its way down and we hear a high-pitched wail
as the hull takes in water on all sides, soaking our shirts

while my friends float away—the fault, of course,
who else's could it be? Lately I've been dreaming too
of tigers gnawing children as if they were dolls,
while I'm in the basement that serves as their den. . . .

Of course it's all about sexual excitement, about
being too close to someone, how I'm consumed by it,
it's my friend gliding down the Mekong with his M-47,
shooting into the trees until he hears the body drop,

a little boy, his surmise, by the shrill pitch of scream,
and God's in there too, the infant God who'll forgive our sins
if we go a little hungry, or how I take my mother to the hospital
for one of her imaginary diseases before she actually dies,

before thank God I'm only one of a thousand lodgers
waking to pigeons on the hotel ledge, looking down
on everyone, blood on the door frame, the traces of
whatever scent I take with me from the night before,

the year before, from centuries before my birth.

Grazing

Sometimes the rapid-fire channel switching is like eye music.
Or when you annihilate an image, another, hydra-like,
appears in its place. Sometimes there's nothing enticing at the malls,
or what we crave is ghostly, far away, long gone.

We have a slim attention span, torn fingernail thin.

They scanned the hillside for the body,
the split-wood fence with barbed wire
where the thrust of my desire was so diffuse
I could almost point to swamp grass and say, yes,
that's what I wanted. One instant bleeding into the next.

You have to imagine the music as random,
dissonant, schizophrenic, playing and not playing,
as if synapses had been cut and sutured back together again.

Where I grew up "getting to know someone"
was alluring, provocative, arresting:
the sheer inventory of body parts, what they indicate,
how they mark a person, dissemble or embolden them.

I can make this personal
and lyrical, if they point the camera
above and behind the ruined individuals, where I can call
the rain-slicked grass emerald green, and beyond that
call out from the granite cliffs, the twisted paths to the sea.

How white her face was, how she disdained
the out-of-doors for all its randomness and contagion.
Her flesh, if we call it flesh, was spongy and doughy, more flexible
than fungible, smudged like newly printed money.

I'm trying to bring you closer.

In the privacy of the hotel room there's a piano
on the radio, the shallow
breathing of someone who's name I won't give you.
My wrist grazing her cheek. Tracing her shoulders, her hips.

What does it mean to be inside
someone else, to feel her hand as a glove your hand wears,
to think her thoughts with and for her . . .
where the body's incited in enactment as well as in metaphor?

For most of an hour we watched them fucking,
in the mirror hotel with the windows open, where happiness
seemed precise, itemized, silent, condensed.
The air they were breathing, we were breathing.

A certain thickness of line becomes them,
where "windows to the soul" cannot be seen.

I have the nagging suspicion that "to be saved"
is all about money, is to save up,
to put on the shelf and savor until maximum value
is accrued. But sometimes the music's

cherubic, the kind Bach's preludes breed
in a practicing child: a fat little angel espousing the cloud.
We're sitting there playing, a little duet, a kettle of steam.

To be watched, inspected, pored over, opened up,
and still receive the adjacent body without turning away
or shutting down: the valve of the door opening
and closing, canting and retracting, as the blood rushes in.

🌿 *Part 2*

How long can we stay interested in the lone man's liberty? I'm afraid, being saved by himself, he will be lost by himself.

—Eugenio Montale

Against Whitman

Too many speak of whip-poor-wills
as if they knew them.
The trout is not my friend.
Oh, I hear a whistling in the trees.
I hear them praying in their tents,
Sunday afternoons. God's creatures:
I don't even know their nesting place.
I suppose I've been a growling dog,
a dusk, a thunderstorm, an ant
creeping up a leg. Spit, testes,
pine sap, sewage, kisses, maple leaf.
God's sopranos, the whip-poor-wills,
sing for hours at a time.
Do you suppose they mate for life?
I hardly know when I'm inside you.
Don't hate the stranger in me.
I also wish the wall of skin
were just another bridge to cross.

The Quake

The quake struck down my father's condo.
As for the soul, the knickknacks rumble a little
and then it's sunny out. And temperate. Except for Disney heirs
and the Gettys, the residents of Pasadena and their Rose Parade.
There's no place for brooding under black umbrellas at the beach.

Exhaust fumes make for pretty sunsets, except for purple splotches
that stained my uncle's forehead. He fell in love with a movie star
and died of AIDS. You might still see him in syndication:
the psychiatrist who explains away mysterious deaths.
We all watch TV: its images have texture and velocity.

If you believe what you see, the dark underbelly of the city
is black with pipes and jewelry, and those who wear
expensive sneakers lounge around in bars,
exchanging vials of crack. When we think of a "mother country,"
perhaps we ask too much: to be taken care of, to be led

to pleasure spots and pain spots a map might indicate in red.
We wore rubber gloves to avoid his spit and blood.
His head was shaved. You've seen people like him: skeletal,
cringing, shivering. His remains are buried near a very pretty vista,
a wrong turn off the freeway, close to the drive-by shootings.

My father wheeled his brother into a hospice,
which had a pool and a spa, tennis courts you had to sign up for.
At the end, one sentence, uttered by anyone, put him to sleep.
But once he memorized *The Tempest* for me, playing all the parts.
He did a credible imitation of the storm that cast the king ashore.

From his portrayal I learned the lesson what animals
we are: graceful and reckless, breakable and luscious.
Gerry died on Tuesday, his voice chalk
on a blackboard. He told jokes till the end, but we
weren't there at the end. Elise died a week ago last Tuesday.

Her breathing stopped suddenly when her lungs collapsed,
her particular pneumonia. Before them, Pablo and Willie,
Lindsay and Drew. Suppose the material world
gives birth to nothing but incongruities, schisms, doubt.
Just as well, then, at the funerals, to invoke St. Catherine,

Esther, and Ruth. Stand-ins, so myths can suffer
for us. All I ask of God's heaven is a mere
intimation, a suspicion, a trifle, a whisper.
Not a flicker of disaster, the mauled flesh snared
in a cavern, the low growl and rumble of the earth.

Izzy

The prettiest shadows were impalpable, so I stored them
in this sentence, where nothing's more than a sequence of words,
thereby degrading them, the scale of gray they cast on the wall,
say, of his parent's bedroom, reduced to a silhouette,
the kind they sold on the Lower East Side to old Jewish families
who could not afford family portraits. Do you feel the pity of it, the boy
making animal shapes on the wall with his fingers, because they had
    nothing,
making the figures dreamy and incandescent, ancient and mythological,
half-man and half-horse, neighing and bucking, mimicking
the boarders' voices in the kitchen? They were building a subway
and wore their mining hats to breakfast, and like him, lived in a tunnel,
inside their own field of vision, meaning all nuances of pain and pleasure
—unless you felt them like a steam iron on your forearm—were
    abstractions,
so as he told me the story, extracting bits of cloth from a moment in 1909,
one from the year preceding, a few after he began working at the cinema,
projecting shadows: Chaplin outwitting a bully,
Keaton escaping a speeding train as his house collapses at his feet—
Izzy's broom shadow to the celluloid swept up and startled into nothing—
I tried to hold everything in place, to draw a picture, since he was half-
    blind by then,

and he had nothing but a string of words to raise us up from—should I say
the tenement?—no, from his wing chair, where I felt like the horse
"shaded" from peripheral view, one who carted him all over the park
so he could sharpen knives, but that was another story, and his face
was no longer draped in lamplight, his face had never been
"draped" in lamplight, but his mouth was shadow, and the tunnel of his
    voice,
as he brought the veil of his hand down over his eyes, gave no sign
the curtain was closing, no sign of how I'd carry on.

I Like Ike

Ike was whispering to his shadow cabinet.
What they called the media back then
was all flashbulbs and phobias.
Earlier, this would bring me to my mother,
but that's like blaming the galaxy
for the burning star consumed by it.
Do I think I'm original? What I wear,
what I say, my complaints, are they not
what they called back then *carbon copies*
of the other sons and daughters of prosperity?

Back then, the statues and the mannequins
modeled for the concrete bunkers
to break the fall of the bomb. I was busy
with my hands in my pockets, looking down
on everyone, because, because it doesn't matter why.
I thought *he* ran the country. We also believed
in crystal balls and cul de sacs, in sexual secrets.
A few cascades and a couple going over the falls in a barrel.
But no one followed them to the bottom.
And we were disappointed when the danger passed.

On the Day of Nixon's Funeral

It's time to put aside the old resentments; lies,
machinations, the paranoia, bugs in telephones,
body bags, secret bombings, his sweaty upper lip,
my cousin Arnie, too dumb to go to school,

too virtuous to confess he'd give blow jobs
for nothing at the Paramount, so he lost a leg
in Da Nang. Now it's time for amnesiacs to play
Beethoven's *Eroica* by Nixon's casket.

To applaud his loyalty, to grant a few mistakes,
to honor his diplomacy, him and his pal Kissinger,
who bombed the lush green paddies of Cambodia.
And now for a few lyric moments as I wait patiently

for my fiftieth birthday. Wood ducks decorate the pond
near this farmhouse, and in the marsh I've spied
a meadowlark, a fox, a white-tailed hawk who soars
above the Western Mountain peaks. Oh, I'm in love

with the country all right. So I can forget my friend
Sweeney, who shot Congressman Lowenstein
because the radio in his tooth insisted on it.
I remember the march on the Pentagon in purple,

a proud member of the Vegetarian Brigade. I was drugged,
as many of us were drugged, as my parents
were drugged by a few major networks, by a ranch house
and an Oldsmobile. I once spit on Hubert Humphrey,

threw a brick through Dow Chemical's plate-glass door.
I wrote insane letters to senators, burying them
in moral rectitude: I got a response from one:
Senator Kennedy—the dead one—whose office wrongly

argued for slow withdrawal instead of Instant Victory.
I remember Tricky Dick in 1953:
I'm eight years old, frightened and ignorant,
lying down before my parents' first TV: my aunts

and uncles sitting in a circle, biting their nails,
whispering names of relatives awaiting trial, who,
thanks to Nixon, lost their sorry jobs. You can see why
I'd want to bury this man whose blood would not circulate,

whose face was paralyzed, who should have died
in shame and solitude, without benefit of eulogy or twenty-one-
gun salutes. I want to bury him in southern California
with the Birchers and the Libertarians. I want to look out

my window and cheer the remaining cedars
that require swampy habitats to survive. To be done
with shame and rage this April afternoon, where embryonic
fiddleheads, fuzzy and curled and pale as wings,

have risen to meet me. After all, they say he was a scrappy man,
wily and sage, who served as Lucifer, scapegoat, scoundrel,
a receptacle for acrimony and rage—one human being
whose life I have no reverence for, which is why I'm singing now.

Vivaldi

This terrified, castrated parasite
spent all day, every day, twelve hours a day,
blackening the page, plagiarizing from himself,
Corelli, Torelli, Scarlatti, anybody
whose voice crossed the courtyards
of the dead Medicis, sucking up to headmasters,
would-be popes, cocks of the walk.
This poseur, this poor obsessive ballless hack,
—four hundred fifty concertos, plus operas and ballets—
this pathetic sop, the "Red priest," who coifed
his hair and powdered his freckled face in mirrors
all over Italy, ran an orphanage for musical girls.
This big-nosed fop, this gossip who in notebooks
took down every slight—he never paid one back—
exhorted his all-girl orchestra to pilfer wine and cheese,
all so you could listen to, and not be harmed,
in malls and barber shops, in the bagel arboretums
of the grazing states like Iowa and Kansas.
You can hear him still, scribbling in the universities,
in high-rise offices, scheming, cajoling, almost making
a living—can you see yourself slaving, pushing papers,
slumped over a loaf of bread and stack of who knows what—
envious and penniless in Topeka, or, better yet, Vienna?

At the Grand Canyon

We were fleeing from the tourists, German and Japanese,
hiking the thick canyon brush, trying to forget
the copperhead sliding between the rocks, sliding toward us

like a florid signature, an old mistake, a trickle of snow
melting off a bridge. Since there is no nature,
since there is no human nature, I suppose we can be done with it,

the whole business of matching trees with moral lessons,
the past set against the future. I'm thinking of a few
right-wing professors who'd blame us for the death of God,

the breakdown of the family. If our individual bodies writhe
in the myth of identity, if the self is not a Roman statue,
then the spirit's nothing but waste. Nevertheless we lumbered

toward lush, spiky vegetation and eroded boulders, tubular
and cavernous, sculpted like a lover's thighs.
Embedded in igneous rock, we found curled-up snails.

And as the trail thinned out, we discovered a plywood hut,
like ones from Los Alamos with dummies seated
at a table sipping tin cups, standing over steam clouds,

mushrooms with a storm bubbling up inside, rattling windows
far west as Salinas. We all need a resurrection or two,
but we did not have a vision—some cheap Christ-like sign

that healed the sky of Hiroshima—when we stood soaking in
the abbreviated light: violet, then charcoal, then bruise,
and finally ebony, until the wind, crackling like torn paper,

cleared out the sky. What followed was a chill that's shadow,
erasure. Then why did we look up—my lover and I—
to get our bearings? You could not call it shame, what called to us

back there, growling in the voice of a grizzly, huddling by a juniper,
burnished and silver, at the crest of the butte. You could see
a blur of light from Vegas, or if you listened closely

you might hear money changing hands, or further back
a few Apache feathers glazed on a necklace. There we were,
caught between two countries: one barbaric and beautiful,

the other spoiled and civilized. As if that were the end of it.

A Missed Opportunity

If Christ slept with the sparrows
he would have heard the same grating cheep
I had to listen to in a Jersey boardinghouse
of prostitution and needlework

where I was trying to sell myself
on the radio, playing jazz all night,
while during the day I knocked on doors
no one would answer, surviving on scallops and soda

(my only account a restaurant). Oh I'd be all right,
in school that fall, planning a lucrative career
in the law, but hardly slept a night
with all that moaning in the room next door.

Even now I keep those voices
in a small compartment with a bare light bulb,
a roach the size of my fist,
and old newspapers with want ads circled in red.

My boss was Mister Roy Cohn,
who cost my aunt and uncle their jobs
in '53. They were Commies, *really*,
who believed in Class Warfare and Revolution

and owned a jewelry store in the Bronx
held up weekly by a few of my neighbors.
I met The Butcher only once, when he fired me,
and went meekly back to the slaughterhouse,

as we called it—someone overdosed once a week—
guilty and ashamed I hadn't made a fucking penny.
Should I have organized my fellow citizens?
Outside, the spotted brown bastards picked up

bread crumbs from the market across the street,
and how they sang for them, reeking
of the gospel, their cheeps all humble and high-pitched,
till a clerk swept them off the sidewalk with a broom.

The Myelogram

for Julius

The purple dye in the needle makes the spine shiver.
    An anesthetic makes it possible to live
with the slackened body, enclosed in a tube, scanned

and catalogued. The pain is bearable. All pain is bearable,
    but that is not the point. Nor is the relativity
of the material world more than a few suicidal philosophers

debating coffee cups in Munich. Then is the surface—
    the metaphor for flesh—mere laminate?
The robe she wore as they wheeled me in was blossoms

and reeds, dreamy verdure, half-consciousness, half-
    willingness to die. The abated body's
flexible, so I was evolving backward: an elephant's trunk,

an eel, a paramecium. What drove me back was *being*,
    beginning inside. The flesh baby pink
at the entrance. All that prodding was clinical: pure

neurological necessity. Doctor Dombronowicz,
    whose Polish family was snuffed
(all of it)—in '44, when Hitler's aides saw

the end to the experiment—told me, "Surgery
     will re-fuse the spine." Or,
"Surgery will refuse the spine." The rejected body:

wheeled out after the operation, was pale enough
     to be bone, chalk, wafer, shell.
Do you know the expression, "A mere shell of himself?"

It was time to say good-bye to those Jews in camps:
     the year I was born Uncle Sidney
was the trope for Treblinka. His declivity, measured skull

and nose, was pure Semitic. You see what nonsense language is,
     how the equation quakes, defending itself
against the needle spear, against the gas etherizing agony?

You can be devoted to pain, or surgically cauterized.
     The doctor knew my uncle, barely.
As a boy he watched him in the orchestra, fiddling Wagner

to Waldheim's regiment. A current runs through the nerve
     conduction test. If the muscles work,
you can't patrol the twitch, but if not it's like being deaf,

like being dead, like being, when love's extracted, like a stitch
     pulled before the wound has healed. As a boy
the doctor was retrieved (no reason given) to save and restore.

What is it about this hesitation, resistance, parenthesis,
     the leap ahead to where it hurt more or less,
when something happened "in kind"? When I came back

to my lover, when the gas began to take effect, I saw
     in that stretched-out haze before
going under, she was beatific (not the real one, sleepless,

outside, wringing her hands with fear), this idea of her,
    her fingers green and tendril-like
so the moment might gleam, leaf-like and tropical,

sheath-like, libidinal, to snag me back, from the kitchen table
    where he'd been sitting, waiting
in a Warsaw boardinghouse, waiting to be taken away:

I came back to put a stop to it, to delete a little history.

Bud Powell at the Club Montmarte, 1961

All of Paris was a hospital.
Doctors stocked revolvers, smoked cigars.
On the black keys he made Chinese music:
stammering, swaying, mumbling,
he saved his better speeches for the piano.

They could not turn out the lights,
so we were lit up, as by Bellows or Grosz,
orange and black, with oval hats,
a red smear of lips. In his suit of white powder,
he was almost flour. I was white

and seventeen, taking notes.
Even after they dressed and made him up,
even after injection after injection
of lithium, he sat at the piano, listening:
his thoughts were severed limbs

sutured to a story. I may have caught
a phrase, a worked-up glance or two,
but Bud was a baby whose hands wandered
over the Left Bank with pock-skinned hookers
who fed him with a spoon. Likewise,

I was happy to suppress the sequence
of sirens, to testify to beauty
before they took him back. I filed away
the residue of melody. But to say
I was happy misconstrues

the boy who hung on every word.
His palms were smoking in his pockets
when he sat down next to me.
"Show me your hands,"
he said. "Your ordinary hands."

Selma

In the sanitary Woolworth's luncheonette,
scent of Pine Sol, scent of hot dog grease, we line up
for oily cups of coffee. While others lean
on hoodless pick-up trucks, line the sleepy dirt-lined streets,

our passion's to disrupt. To sit, because
where people walk their daily miles to church,
faith in the gospel's palpable as dusk—so I empty
my pocketful of change, the manager shakes

with rage, customers turn their pale faces,
and we sit and wait to be served. All this doubleness
rubs against me like flint on brick, like a club
rapped on a kneecap, dropping me to prayer.

Slipping into the skin of the other,
to the back-of-the-bus other, to the pork rind
and steamed greens other, may be
a matter of enterprise, a sizing up, a seance

where God speaks to us just once,
in the voice of a preacher. And if I learn nothing
of the hero's hallelujah, of the power
of boundless faith: if I can't digest two hot dogs

and a bitter cup of coffee before a yapping
German shepherd nips my leg, I believe,
when so absorbed, the self leaks out of things,
to join the bath of voices calling, the clapping hands.

I bask in it. The bloodbath, a steamy pot above the meal.

Don't Cry for Me, Argentina

Where I've never been, my head is full
of amputations. Perón shoots out a few windows:
the whole schoolhouse is red pen mistaken.
Time and space have no place on the Pampas
where the slit throat of a horse

pays for a dumb suggestion. Storytellers of America,
stay away from poetry. Sequence lovers, defenders
of syntax and symmetry, it's winter there
when it blisters here, and when I'm sluggish,
torpid, the density of me

thick as a block of ice, when
my head's a traffic jam, spiked
with shards of glass at the intersection
of fill-in-the-blank, they're burning clapboards
in a barn to warm their hands. The lost earring

in the rafters slips through the slats,
so the cowboy remembers her breath sifting
through the gauzy shirt, the heat of falling asleep
under a lamp. And while Madonna's
lip-synching Eva Perón, I'm thinking spangles

and cattle prod when a few thousand dissidents
are piped in to a mountain retreat to be hung. That's where
the cowboy, who wrote a poem on the inside band of his hat,
brings, in writing, the earring back: his neck
will break for it.

There's No Rigor like the Old Rigor

Was it something uncleaved, clean-cut you wanted?
Something cheerleader, vacuumed, clean-shaven?
Before the truck stop marred stands of cedar. Before father
succumbed to the secretary, scribbled a note or two on his tie?

It says something about us
that we no longer read Ovid. Of course,

some don't like to be shunned, stepped on,
spurned, excluded, don't like to be shuttled back and forth
between the barge and the mansion, serving him
hot milk while he reads Stendhal by the fire.
They like to be admired, chauffeured, they like silver,
they like to be stirred, to stray from the herd,
called not just when they're needed but missed.

You wanted something whole. One God.
What's wrong with that? In the paintings, the Gods
are happy. Why shouldn't they be? Beauty
had a certain volume. The cracked foot of the statue David.
When windows were still church windows,
before stained-glass would disintegrate into slag and gravel
if you brought back the blitzkreig, those shiny pornographic photos. . . .

Lingerie shred in the hall. A party
you hardly remember.
It was like this. You had a few ideas about women.
A few women gave you ideas.
But why indulge in the shattered lampshade,
the painting askew on the inner wall?
What matters is what always mattered.
Standards. The stations of the cross. Grace. The good
shucked from the bad with a good sharp knife.
The time before the the. The first time. The first wife.

Overheard

The shadowy cormorants came from someone else's voice.
So a voice can be effaced, gagged, overtaken, rebuked.
We hear the song of *the* phoebe and *the* chickadee.
My wife's scream was so familiar, etc.
I wracked my brain, motherfucker. We cater
to all kinds. Then how do I know
the *I* who said it? When we turn the TV on,

strangers do the talking. In Nicaragua, I witnessed
suffering unparalleled, followed by examples.
Let's get personal, she said.
I want to know what sound that bruise will make
when I touch it. Guttural, hoarse, various
volume, pitch, and tone? When he turns eleven
Casey will say, *My voice is changing*, as if

he were solitary. We saw some blackbirds in bright sunlight,
if you want to get technical, and I couldn't explain
what flew over me darkly, the range of it

and speed before the utterance, how moved
I'd been, and before that, how distressed.
So we put our calm voices on and sat down
Platonic-like, like statues on the wharf, as if waiting for someone

to tell us to Keep a Move On. The cop with the voice
of a horse's hoof on macadam, who tapped my shoe with his billy club.

Eternity

You can almost taste it,
twist it, roll it up into a ball, watch it sulk in the corner,
bring it a vodka and tonic, listen to its sad story:

something had knocked it off a shelf,
sent it reeling, kept it from getting there on time,
from setting up and taking things out of their boxes on the lawn. . . .

It must be elastic, this invisible hiatus, this parenthesis,
the dim prospect we ponder, shape our destinies around,
pray to, approximate in sex or endless hours at the register

waiting for the boss to let us go, just before we can talk to him,
just before we can straighten out a misunderstanding or two. Endings
are bad signs. Even detours at the broken-down suspension bridge

when you're hurrying home, when he's lying there
tied to machines, or when she's on the edge
of it for hours, his tongue dangling there and teasing,

the nerve endings raw, shattered with excitement,
when the truth is nothing but a paltry, cavernous impulse
to fix what's broken. Once I caught a trace of it,

embedded in a fox's skull on the ridge of Electric Peak
in the Grand Tetons. Of course it was storming, and the bright
jagged lightning forks burned holes in the ore-infested earth.

Inside it, though, a nubble of green moss
the texture of a mushroom cap was sprouting: the skull
in the shape of a butte, air surrounding it, whistling in the sockets.

❦ *Part 3*

Poetry is a satisfying of the desire for resemblance.
—Wallace Stevens

Or ever the silver cord be loosed, or the golden bowl
be broken, or the pitcher be broken at the fountain, or
the wheel broken at the cistern—
—Ecclesiastes

Delirious

It's all savagery and appropriation,
all butt-fucking and scarring faces with broken bottles,
buying a new Toyota to ape the neighbors,

it's all coughing in the cities, feces in the rivers,
a few old gossips in the Laundromat,
a wrinkled magazine where a neighbor's suddenly famous,

it's all a welt on the baby's forehead, a mirror
for the greasy corned beef sandwich on East Thirty-Fourth,
and then it's not. Then it's Linda and me

trailing through the country, a noisy Casey
and Julie behind us, then it's the snowbells seeping
through the muddy riverbank, and the stream finding its way

to the sewer, and then it's being attached to the sea
at dusk, the murky afflatus of water,
violet and copper, the picture window framing the harbor,

before we're floating downriver, a little serenade
from the terns and the pines
smudged charcoal in reflection. You don't want to hear

about my happiness. It amounts to one person for a minute
walking through a park, the same park
whose momentary blooms—the shrub rose with saw-tooth leaves,

its green thorns spiking the dew, the flimsy petals,
palm-like, somewhere between violet
and pink, like skin scraped raw—could make him cringe.

It's dark by now, so we can close the doors
whose hinges seem to be crying
to infuse a little emotion in the privacy of our apartments,

where we're sacred individuals, gorging our urgent body parts
in blood and screams, no longer willing
to shave the hair off chimpanzees, to attach them to wires

to see how we behave, and yet, and yet, and yet . . .

An Improbable Delirium

An improbable delirium brings me
to the jack pines with their scrubby peeling bark,
roots sprouting out of granite, their twisted branches

half-gnawed, so in the sea breeze
they mutter as they batter and withdraw,
before swaying like a plane that misses a runway,

brushing over the forest, scaring everyone
with that chalk-on-blackboard sound,
the scorched half-syllables of calamitous pain.

Something tells me it's the job of poetry
to bring some wretched character out on stage,
to gesture wildly, giving a soliloquy

we carry with us to the sea, the sea
that absorbs us and wants us to forget
where we came from, that high-pitched

chop and spume, turgid surges
that stir the murky surface into ebony.
There's something cobalt about us,

not just squalid, murky, bedraggled:
Someone had to teach us to be timorous,
naked and throbbing as a jellyfish,

but less translucent, more transparent.
Until the end, when we're indecipherable,
composed, seraphic, speechless.

The Depression

A critical mass came over me.
All those little things we do for ourselves—
chocolate bars, a clean shirt, good books, my favorite pew
at church—were suddenly unavailable.

Coming home was opening the vault.
Someone was sitting on me. The welt
was inside my forehead. Motion was a concept,
like algebra. In other words I was adjacent

to the maelstrom: I won't take it away
by effacing it: it was no cloudy day in November.
It was raucous, with all my pliable desires
going nowhere: I was modeling clay.

You can't figure it out, she said.
Should I thank psychoanalysis for that?
The current lingo's all immersion, self-sufficiency,
dredging up the dark and staring into it. Later,

maybe decades later, we'll laugh at the gall of it.
Since for no good reason, the she I wanted came to me.
I thought of the shiny ebony of a Steinway.
Pedals. Then petals, peeling back. Then the prattling stopped.

All the familiar figures abandoned me. You see, I was all along
unprepared for the stillness that accompanies happiness.

The Annunciation

Berkeley, 1992

Is everything we want shielded,
sheathed, and stored away? A few shafts of light
in a storeroom, dust motes in the attic

of someone else's story? For years I tossed in bed,
the shame sweating from me, saturated with fever,
coughing up a few syllables caught in my throat.

Long after the roses had released their petals
and thorns, when the eucalyptus was peeling back
its scent of cat piss, I said good-bye to everyone.

There's nothing *like* the self-pity of the unloved,
watching the world desiccate and deplete
like an apricot rolled under a stove. But there she was,

my own infinity, mirror to the vault
I looked out from, across the street
where the plant was boarded up, where a few windows

reflected a mauve stupidity, all that squandered labor.
Don't you hate metaphors? How they phony up
correspondence, so one shrill noise is like another,

when words are stand-ins, being *beside*
instead of *inside*. Except the window opened
when no one opened it. I felt that flush

of the fecal and ecstatic mixing the cloudy air
above the industrial city. I sank down
in that sweaty splinter of a pit in the first person,

listening to the measure of my own breathing,
until I drifted down, taken by sooty flecks of air
to the paradise of the she who wants me,

where there are no words to spare.
You can pity me, but back then I was walking on coals
and burning: I was a furnace and every scrap went into it.

The Martyrs

for L.C.

They were so sick and tired
they hardly knew they were fucking.
His body ached and pulsed: breathing

was a labor. Sweating too, his forehead
dripping on her forehead, so with her palm
she swept his brow. That's when

he looked down, took in the abyss
of her face—no, the gulf was his—her face
was full, open, her fleshy cheeks

flushed pink with asphyxiation.
Many years' pleasure had been denied them.
But now they were sunlight, hot

and shining, not yards from the cliff
where surf kicked up and crows were cawing,
where St. Sebastian had stopped singing.

They were all steam and cloud,
evaporate: a site of wreckage, fever, limbs
as twisted wings, unappeasable beauty.

Just so, they hovered above their combustible bodies.

The Rapture

The tongue wagging, mumbling and moaning,
calling out, shouting instructions, legs buckling, scalding
where the flesh grinds against flesh, the veil

of seduction dropped, the quick and shallow breathing
(outside, truck tires whistling, a child on a bike,
but muffled, as if the gagged world were boiled down

to liquid, capped, pharmeceutical, a store
where sickness is soothed), then the acquired things:
this borrowed from what she did with someone else,

that from what he once saw, this from magazines,
the once shamed and detonated flesh now truculent
and delectable, then the seizure, the moment

nothing more than rapid eye movement,
mere transparency, followed by declarations
and a snail-like withdrawal, the dreaded afterwards,

the schism and the questions, the heart
beginning to stutter and calm, space coming back
into focus, coming back too quickly:

the night table, the book, the clock,
everything that refuses to change pulsing with solidity.
Then it's back: the anonymous clutter of the avenue,

ravenous looks reflected in every storefront
so nothing's left but a flash of body part,
a sensation dimly lit, scored like film and fluttering.

I Join the Sparrows

Let me join the sparrows
in the snow. As one of them,
I'd stir the kingdom up
and to their busy fluttering
add a chirp. If I could
make a sound to satisfy
the heavens, like wind
through paper, a harp
of wings, if I could join
the kingdom of the startled
constantly, I'd lose the snow-
capped mountain view,
the death I earned, laboring.
God, speak to me
through sparrows, insist
we're not waste and water.
The sunlight fading
late December holds no lesson
for the living. Perched
on earthly wings, above
the bog where sparrows mate
and make their home,
I'd sing awhile, a high, faint trill.

I Like Waking Up

I like waking up by the lake
frozen over, the frosty meadow
where a white horse still huffs and chafes
by the fence post and a few fog clouds
cling to the tree line of the Sugar Loaf range.
I like the lake a block of ice. A few years ago
I would have said *paralyzed*,
but I didn't live where Linda wakes now,
her children lightly breathing a wall away.
And until a logging truck trudges by
on our dirt road—its chains rattling—
we have a moment together. I'd like to say
the world began this way: on the cusp
of winter: Five A.M.,
no gunshots, no sickly deer
limping asymmetrically
into the clearing. Before still water
turned to gnats and mosquitoes,
the algaed pond that murky, turquoise green
we make of things.

At the Movies

for Kenny

An October drive through the leaf parade:
blood reds, pumpkin yellows with a cast of green.
Whatever's knocking around inside has opened the shutters

and gone for a walk. Common stuff suddenly blazes
in particular: you know how you put off
the optometrist, trying to deny your diminished vision,

but the new glasses brought clarity to your whole life,
meaning definition and composition, shape
and structure? That's how I feel about the movies.

Maybe there's an afterlife already composed of
our favorite scenes, a harp concerto by Handel, a plate full
of granted wishes. Maybe our spirits just loom

eternally, with a doctrine full of footnotes untangling
natural disasters, stillborn children, and history's
handful of malice. Still, I'll take my chances with my eyes

open wide in this dark place, consuming images
in the pews of someone else's choosing. Of course my taste
is cheap, corrupted by greed, TV, a compulsiveness

and fear of desolation just vast enough to be conceived.
But you can't convince me heaven satisfies
more than *That Obscure Object of Desire*, where everyone

waits forever to be served. Secondly, suffering's
formless, unjustifiable, saturated with shame
and an art based on resignation and hate. Whereas

On Golden Pond, filmed a few short miles from here,
phony as a sermon on the virtues of the family,
transformed an inconsolable death into miracle,

and once gave me a place to grieve and rest my feet.

Language

It's all talk isn't it, emblem
and suggestion, it's either tremulous stutter
or taunting display: flashy but fleshless, a con man
plotting his way out of a ticket, concocting a story
to conquer and seduce. Once removed,

it's safer to be the figure than the feeling.
On the whale watch I hid in the hold
because I didn't want the awe to wash over me—
so I scribbled *the raven, cormorant, and gull,*
archaic signs, obsolete, archeological fragments,

a cursive you can almost witness, can't you?
A few scrawls of letters among millions. And if
the scatterbrained are speechless, as mother said,
if their mouths are voiceless, unemployed,
their breath won't spark a mirror. Once removed

I know I'll want to edit, take everything back,
revise, inspect, freeze the event and diminish it
with particulars. Trade the fog bank for a buttress
of seaweed. Struck by the wheeze of the fluke,
I listened to the patter of sailors coasting on breakers,

to how the skittish engine chattered and stalled
and I want to say clamored, for that's how close I was
to the motor humming. Oh I know, talk is cheap. Tawdry,
specious, a source of distance and misunderstanding,
probative and salacious: lustrous too, if I say so.

The Inner Life

I'm jittery, sleepless, I hover over a chair
instead of nesting in it. I live for a few bites of chocolate,
my hand grazing her hair. The inner life
excites me unbearably, listening to a woman
grind her teeth, finding out what makes her slap her husband,
what makes a job a treadmill, what charms me about the neck scent,
why do we pour everything out, as if ears were the swirl of a drain?

I live for the jabbering auctioneer,
his lips like the wake from a canoe on Lake Witaka,
selling a canopy bed where grandma
told grandpa a terrible secret. She lived in the desert once.
In 1933 she slept in a railroad car.
Where is she now, the one who ran off with a seamstress?

I could live with a few more hot baths, inspecting
the sweat as steam infuses the skin, inhaling and exhaling it
like a Santa Ana. Before it rains, I think of kettles of tea.
A few Polish aunts and uncles fighting over the Talmud
while comparing stitches on the linen tablecloth.

My people crossed the desert, all the while chattering
"How unbearable the heat, how thirsty we are."
Those are not my people. My people are thinking
what a joy to slash the throat of an enemy. My people
stole leftover sandwich crusts from the Automat.

I want to live a few more minutes
for my people, the ones who say, *Call me*
sounding like crows on the side of a highway
when no raccoon decorates the interstate.
I live for a few more minutes of the inner thigh.
To make up for skulking around with my eyes closed,
believing the God of pain a private thing.
Ennobling. I have a few meals in mind.
My people love to feed, to inject pleasure and pain,
to wound or annihilate, to comb
and burnish the flesh so we can strut and preen.

The thingness of us. Going off like a buzzer
in a factory, where we charge out the doors denouncing
the one who sticks his head in a stack of papers
then comes out shrugging, giving us the thumb.
They're going to Mexico without us. To the beaches
and factories, to the piñatas and dreidel-sized milagras
of severed arms, goddesses and crosses. Mexico,

a country without statutes,
where they fit tiny chips on a board with tweezers,
then do it again and again. Nothing but a few
greased-up windows, a picnic table in a chain-linked yard
where a Doberman slobbers and growls. To be looked at

like that, inspected, to miss the surf and the streetcars,
that's what hell is. When they're working harder,
cheaper. Talking in another language. Hiding their faces.

I don't want to live in a cave. I want to hear
what they're saying. My ear's to the wall
with a glass, I'm shushing everyone. My people
don't need a god to make speeches about shedding the flesh:
we want to get on with it, to be the seismographs
who register sensations, who store them in a vase
like a key to the cellar. To be the ones who open
the basement door with its smell of mold and enchilada,
who make out the first notes of the mariachi band,
the steel guitars, who think red and black
silk crinolines, just when our eyes adjust to the darkness.

Illinois Poetry Series

Laurence Lieberman, Editor

The Floating Candles
Sydney Lea (1982)

Northbook
Frederick Morgan (1982)

Collected Poems, 1930-83
Josephine Miles (1983)

The River Painter
Emily Grosholz (1984)

Healing Song for the Inner Ear
Michael S. Harper (1984)

The Passion of the Right-Angled Man
T. R. Hummer (1984)

Dear John, Dear Coltrane
Michael S. Harper (1985)

Poems from the Sangamon
John Knoepfle (1985)

In It
Stephen Berg (1986)

The Ghosts of Who We Were
Phyllis Thompson (1986)

Moon in a Mason Jar
Robert Wrigley (1986)

Lower-Class Heresy
T. R. Hummer (1987)

Poems: New and Selected
Frederick Morgan (1987)

Furnace Harbor: A Rhapsody of the
   North Country
Philip D. Church (1988)

Bad Girl, with Hawk
Nance Van Winckel (1988)

Blue Tango
Michael Van Walleghen (1989)

Eden
Dennis Schmitz (1989)

Waiting for Poppa at the Smithtown
   Diner
Peter Serchuk (1990)

Great Blue
Brendan Galvin (1990)

What My Father Believed
Robert Wrigley (1991)

Something Grazes Our Hair
S. J. Marks (1991)

Walking the Blind Dog
G. E. Murray (1992)

The Sawdust War
Jim Barnes (1992)

The God of Indeterminacy
Sandra McPherson (1993)

Off-Season at the Edge of the World
Debora Greger (1994)

Counting the Black Angels
Len Roberts (1994)

Oblivion
Stephen Berg (1995)

To Us, All Flowers Are Roses
Lorna Goodison (1995)

Honorable Amendments
Michael S. Harper (1995)

Points of Departure
Miller Williams (1995)

Dance Script with Electric Ballerina
Alice Fulton (reissue, 1996)

To the Bone: New and Selected Poems
Sydney Lea (1996)

Floating on Solitude
Dave Smith (3-volume reissue, 1996)

Bruised Paradise
Kevin Stein (1996)

Walt Whitman Bathing
David Wagoner (1996)

Rough Cut
Thomas Swiss (1997)

Paris
Jim Barnes (1997)

The Ways We Touch
Miller Williams (1997)

The Rooster Mask
Henry Hart (1998)

The Trouble-Making Finch
Len Roberts (1998)

Grazing
Ira Sadoff (1998)

National Poetry Series

Eroding Witness
Nathaniel Mackey (1985)
Selected by Michael S. Harper

Palladium
Alice Fulton (1986)
Selected by Mark Strand

Cities in Motion
Sylvia Moss (1987)
Selected by Derek Walcott

The Hand of God and a Few Bright Flowers
William Olsen (1988)
Selected by David Wagoner

The Great Bird of Love
Paul Zimmer (1989)
Selected by William Stafford

Stubborn
Roland Flint (1990)
Selected by Dave Smith

The Surface
Laura Mullen (1991)
Selected by C. K. Williams

The Dig
Lynn Emanuel (1992)
Selected by Gerald Stern

My Alexandria
Mark Doty (1993)
Selected by Philip Levine

The High Road to Taos
Martin Edmunds (1994)
Selected by Donald Hall

Theater of Animals
Samn Stockwell (1995)
Selected by Louise Glück

The Broken World
Marcus Cafagña (1996)
Selected by Yusef Komunyakaa

Nine Skies
A. V. Christie (1997)
Selected by Sandra McPherson

Lost Wax
Heather Ramsdell (1998)
Selected by James Tate

Other Poetry Volumes

Local Men and *Domains*
James Whitehead (1987)

Her Soul beneath the Bone:
  Women's Poetry on Breast Cancer
Edited by Leatrice Lifshitz (1988)

Days from a Dream Almanac
Dennis Tedlock (1990)

Working Classics: Poems on Industrial
  Life
Edited by Peter Oresick and Nicholas Coles
  (1990)

Hummers, Knucklers, and Slow Curves:
  Contemporary Baseball Poems
Edited by Don Johnson (1991)

The Double Reckoning of Christopher
  Columbus
Barbara Helfgott Hyett (1992)

Selected Poems
Jean Garrigue (1992)

New and Selected Poems, 1962-92
Laurence Lieberman (1993)